What happens when you

THINK?

WHAT HAPPENS WHEN ... ?

Library of Congress Cataloging-in-Publication Data

Richardson, Joy.
   What happens when you think?

   (What happens when — ?)
   Bibliography: p.
   Includes index.
   Summary: Describes how the brain works and how this complex and
powerful organ interacts with other parts of the body to receive and
transmit messages.
   1. Thought and thinking—Juvenile Literature. [1. Brain.   2. Thought
and thinking] I. Maclean, Colin, 1930-   .   II. Maclean, Moira.
III. Title.   IV. Series: Richardson, Joy. What happens when — ?
BF455.R465   1986   153.4'2   86-1934

ISBN 1-55532-138-0
ISBN 1-55532-113-5 (lib. bdg.)

This North American edition first published in 1986 by
Gareth Stevens, Inc.
7221 West Green Tree Road Milwaukee, Wisconsin 53223, USA

U.S. edition, this format, copyright ©1986
Supplementary text and illustrations copyright ©1986
by Gareth Stevens, Inc.
Illustrations copyright ©1985 by Colin and Moira Maclean

First published in the United Kingdom by Hamish Hamilton Children's
Books with an original text copyright by Joy Richardson.
Typeset by: Ries Graphics, ltd.
Series editor: MaryLee Knowlton
Cover design: Gary Moseley
Additional illustration/design: Laurie Shock

What happens when you
THINK?

Joy Richardson

pictures by
Colin and Moira Maclean

introduction by
Gail Zander, Ph.D.

Gareth Stevens Publishing
Milwaukee

... a note to parents and teachers

Curiosity about the body begins shortly after birth when babies explore with their mouths. Gradually children add to their knowledge through sight, sound, and touch. They ask questions. However, as they grow, confusion or shyness may keep them from asking questions, and they may acquire little knowledge about what lies beneath their skin. More than that, they may develop bad feelings about themselves based on ignorance or misinformation.

The *What Happens When ... ?* series helps children learn about themselves in a way that promotes healthy attitudes about their bodies and how they work. They learn that their bodies are systems of parts that work together to help them grow, stay well, and function. Each book in the series explains and illustrates how one of the systems works.

With the understanding of how their bodies work, children learn the importance of good health habits. They learn to respect the wonders of the body. With knowledge and acceptance of their bodies' parts, locations, and functions, they can develop a healthy sense of self.

This attractive series of books is an invaluable source of information for children who want to learn clear, correct, and interesting facts about how their bodies work.

GAIL ZANDER, Ph.D.
CHILD PSYCHOLOGIST
MILWAUKEE PUBLIC SCHOOLS

Your brain is very clever
and very complicated.
It controls your whole body.
It learns and remembers and thinks.
Nobody knows exactly how it works.

Your brain is not very big.

Put a ribbon around your eyebrows
and down over your ears.
Tie it at the back of your neck.

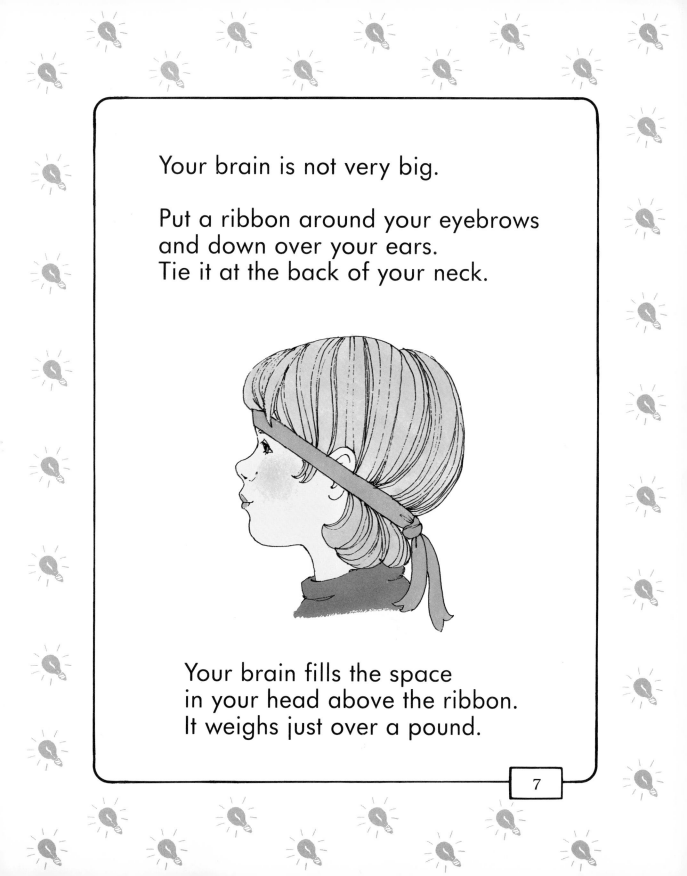

Your brain fills the space
in your head above the ribbon.
It weighs just over a pound.

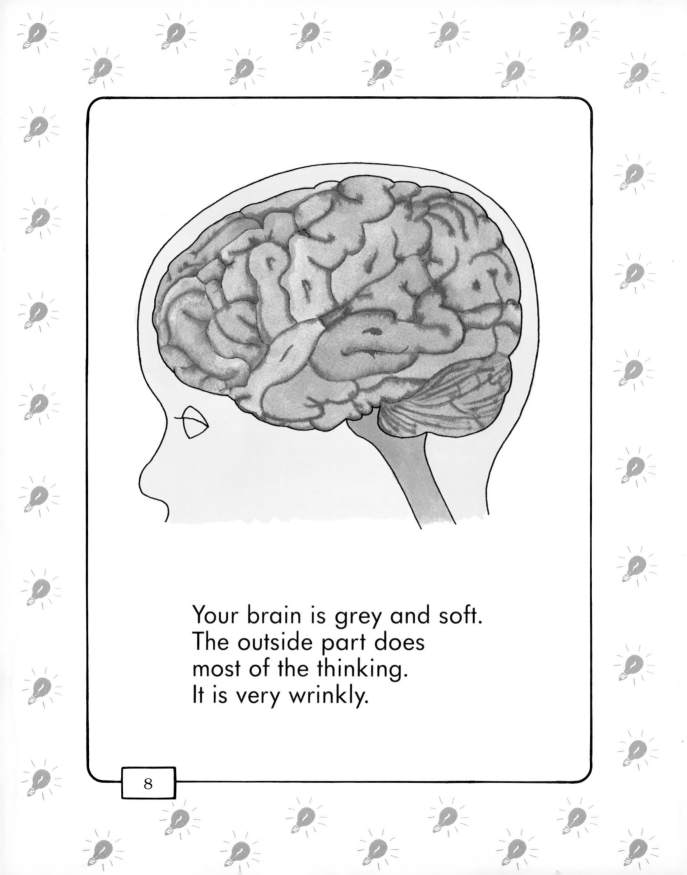

Your brain is grey and soft.
The outside part does
most of the thinking.
It is very wrinkly.

Wrinkle up a page of newspaper.
Ask a friend to put
the fingers of both hands
together to make a cage
about the size of your brain.
Can you fit the newspaper into it?

The wrinkles in your brain
make a large thinking area
fit into a small space.

Long thin threads called nerves carry messages between your brain and every part of your body.

Your nerves are made of cells. Messages pass along your nerves from one cell to the next.

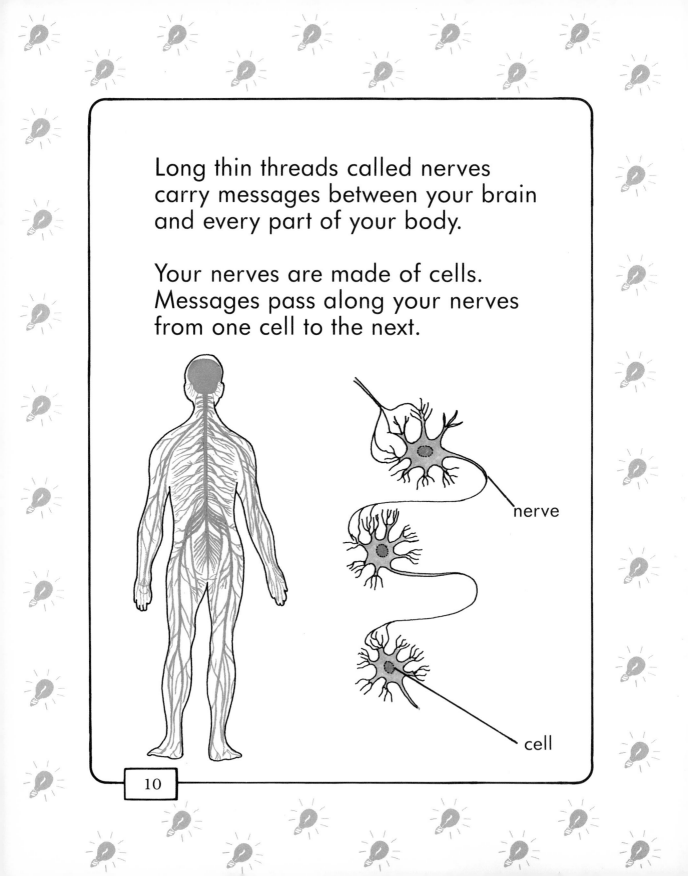

nerve

cell

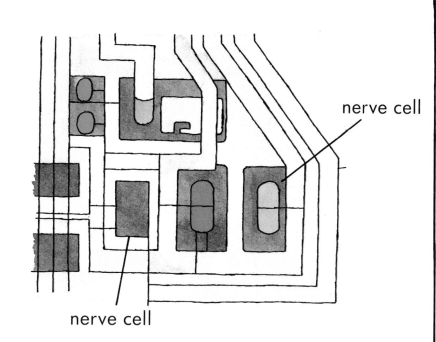

nerve cell

nerve cell

Your brain is made of millions
and millions of tiny nerve cells.

Each nerve cell is
linked up to lots of others,
sort of like the inside of a computer.

Messages pass along special routes
to get to different parts of your brain.

Your brain has two halves.
They are joined in the middle.

Messages from the right side
of your body go to the
left side of your brain.

Messages from the left side
of your body go to the
right side of your brain.

Pick up a pencil.
Which hand did you use?
Look through a hollow tube.
Which eye did you use?
Kick a ball.
Which foot did you use?

Most people use one side of their
bodies more than the other.
If you are left-handed,
the right side of your brain is bigger.
That's because it has more to do.
If you are right-handed,
the left side of your brain is bigger.

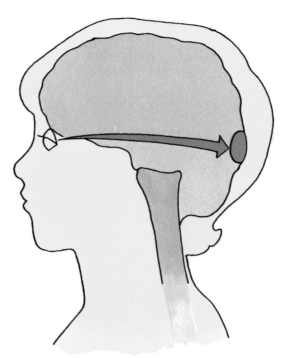

Messages from your eyes go
to the back of your brain.
Your brain turns the
messages into pictures.
Your eyes cannot work
without your brain.

Messages from your ears go
to the side of your brain.
Your brain decides which sounds
to listen to.
It shuts off other sounds so that
you do not notice them.

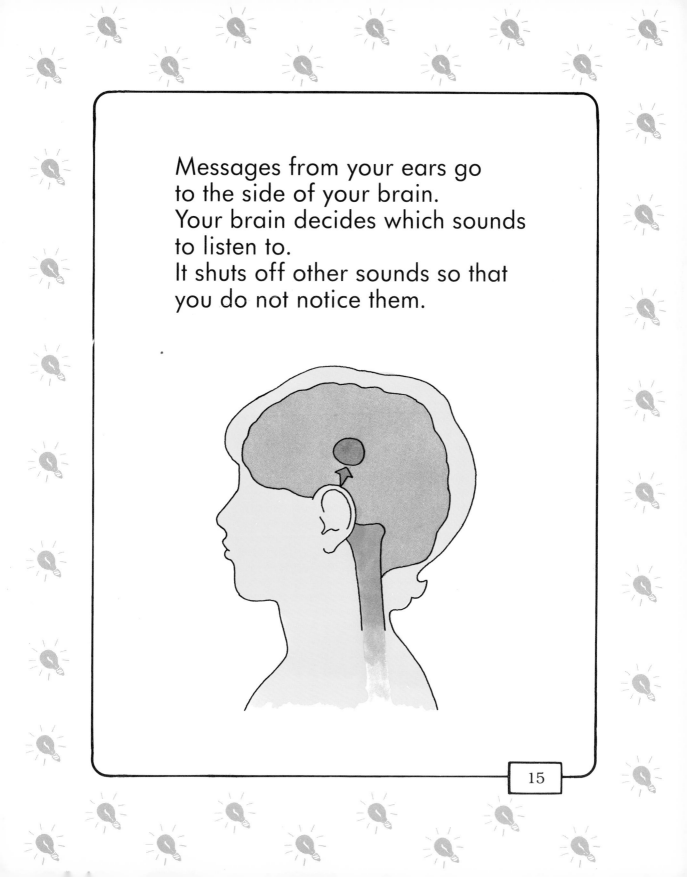

Your skin picks up messages about
the things you touch and feel.

The messages go to a special strip
in the middle of your brain.
Your hands and your mouth
do the most feeling.
So they need the most brain space.

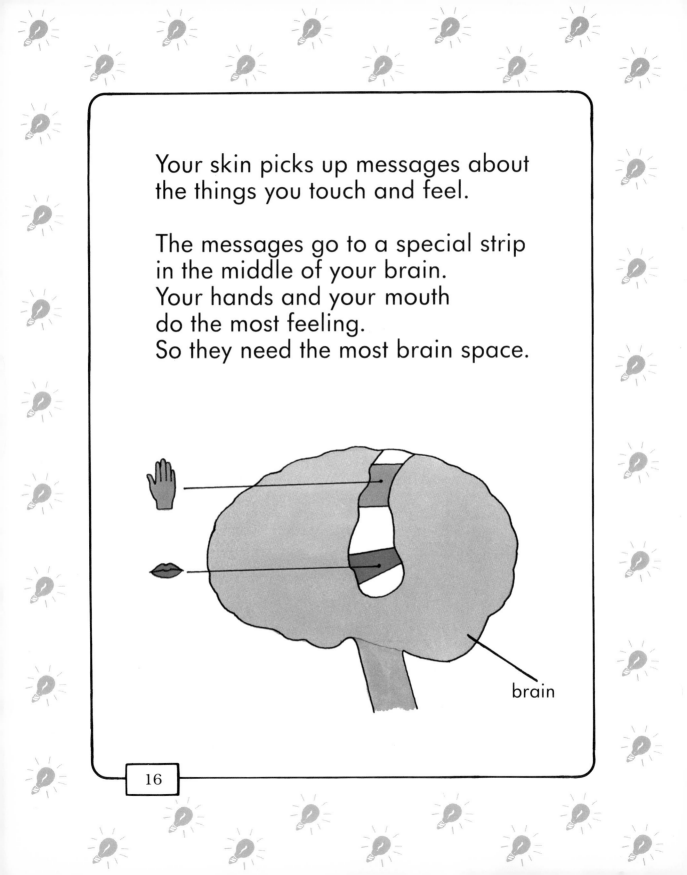

brain

New messages keep coming into
your brain.
But you can only think
about one at a time.

Stop reading and sit still.
What can you see?
What can you hear?
What can you feel?

While you were concentrating on
reading, your brain stopped the other
messages from crowding into your mind.

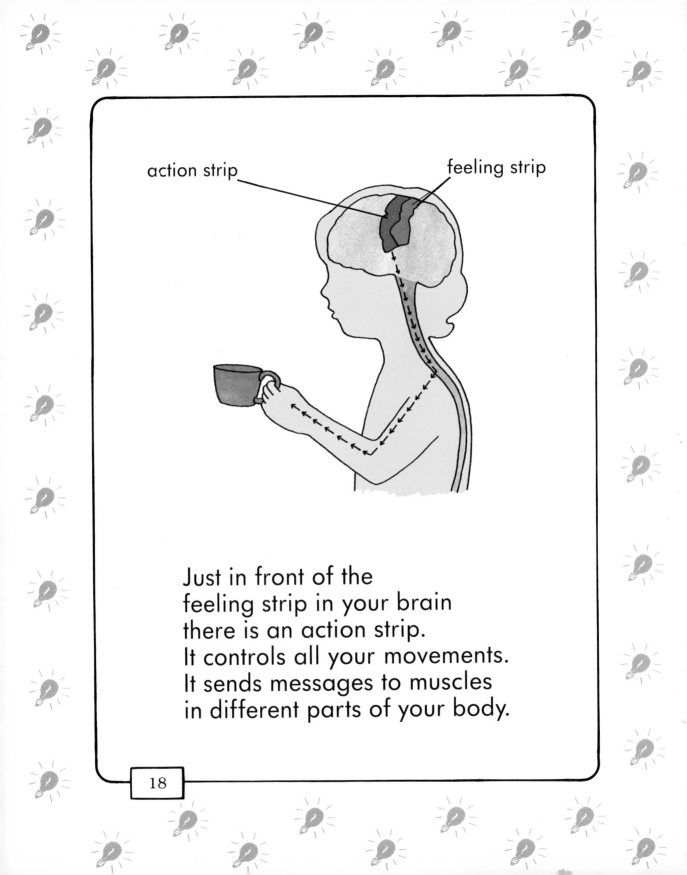

action strip

feeling strip

Just in front of the
feeling strip in your brain
there is an action strip.
It controls all your movements.
It sends messages to muscles
in different parts of your body.

Stand up!
Smile!
Walk across the room!

Your brain tells your muscles what
to do.
You do not have to think about it.

When you learn to swim
or ride a bicycle,
your brain remembers
the new movements.

If you have to choose
a dessert from a plate,
your brain sees the desserts.
It remembers their tastes.
It figures out the one
you want most and
makes your hand pick it up.

Large parts of your brain are used
for putting thoughts together.
Your brain makes thoughts
from things you see and hear
and feel and remember.

Your brain stores information
in your memory so that
you can use it again later.

Think of someone you have not
seen for a long time.
Count how many things you can
still remember about him or her.

Some information only stays in
your memory for a short time.

Ask a friend to say five numbers
(such as 3 — 9 — 7 — 4 — 6).
Can you repeat them
in the same order?
Now count to a hundred.
Can you still remember the numbers?

You cannot remember everything
forever.
Your brain would have
too much work to do.

You use your memory for learning.

Find a word you cannot spell.
Look at it carefully.
Look at the difficult parts.

Now cover up the word.
Can you write it from memory?

When you learn to spell a word,
your brain makes a picture of it
to keep in your memory.

Take a quick look
at these two pictures.
Try to draw them from memory.

It is easy to remember
things that make sense.
It is difficult to remember
things you do not understand.

Can you do this problem?

A boy had eight gumdrops.
He ate three and gave two away.
How many were left?

Your brain had to think clearly
to turn the words into numbers
and figure out the right answer.

Sometimes you daydream.
Marvelous pictures and exciting ideas
come into your mind.

When you read a story,
or write one yourself,
you make your own pictures
inside your head.

Animals can think.
They can think about what
they see and hear and feel.
But your brain can do more.
It can think about
what happens when you think!

How Does That Happen?

Did you find all these things to do in *What Happens When You THINK?* If not, turn back to the pages listed here and have some fun seeing how your body works.

1. Wrap a ribbon around your brain. (page 7)
2. Measure the size of a brain. (page 9)
3. Which hand do you use most? (page 13)
4. See what was going on while you were reading. (page 17)
5. What does your brain tell your muscles? (page 19)
6. Count the things you remember about someone you haven't seen for a long time. (page 22)
7. Play a number memory game. (page 23)
8. Teach yourself to spell a new word. (page 24)
9. Play a drawing memory game. (page 25)
10. Play an arithmetic game. (page 26)

More Books About Thinking

Listed below are more books about what happens when you think. If you are interested in them, check your library or bookstore.

About Your Brain. Simon/Kendrick (McGraw-Hill)
The Brain and Nervous System. Ward (Franklin Watts)
From Head to Toes: How Your Body Works. Packard (Simon & Schuster)
Happy Healthkins: A Book About Mental Health. Moncure (Childrens Press)
My Sister's Special. Prall (Childrens Press)
She's My Sister: Having a Retarded Sister. Miner (Crestwood House)
Use Your Brain. Showers (Harper & Row)
Why Are Some People Left-Handed? Haislet (Creative Education)
Your Brain and How It Works. Zim (Morrow)
Your Busy Brain. McNamara/Litchfield (Little, Brown)

Where to Find More About Thinking

Here are some people you can write away to for more information about what happens when you think. Be sure to tell them exactly what you want to know about. Include your full name and address so they can write back to you.

National Association for Mental Health
1800 North Kent Street
Arlington, Virginia 22209

United Cerebral Palsy Associations, Inc.
66 East 34th Street
New York, New York 10016

Index